The Winning Mind

The Winning Mind

*How to Turn Your Stumbling
Blocks into Building Blocks*

Reindorf O. Bempah

authorHOUSE®

AuthorHouse™ UK Ltd.
1663 Liberty Drive
Bloomington, IN 47403 USA
www.authorhouse.co.uk
Phone: 0800.197.4150

Published by AuthorHouse   10/14/2014

ISBN: 978-1-4918-9023-3 (sc)
ISBN: 978-1-4918-9022-6 (hc)
ISBN: 978-1-4918-9024-0 (e)

Contents

About Author

 Reindorf O. Bempah holds a Bachelor of Arts Degree in Family Counseling from Central University College, Ghana and a Diploma in Integrated Theology from the Faith Sanctuary Bible Institute an affiliate to Rochester Christian Ministries International, New York,

USA. He has over 13 years experience in Pastoral ministry. In addition, he interned in counseling at the Domestic Violence and Victim support unit at the Ghana Police Department, Ministries Accra.

Reindorf writes and speaks on faith, motivational insights and leadership topics with churches, youth organizations and corporate Leaders. As a respected role model, he shares timeless life principles and bible based success principles that guarantee world-class results to individuals and organizations worldwide on his blog "Success World" where he shares thought-provoking, life-transforming and cutting-edge secrets to successful living via http:// reindorfarticle.bloggspot.com. His "Wisdom Pills" articles are read by over 800 organizational leaders, changing minds, provoking thoughts and impacting the lives of many.

His passion is to help and develop people to live a life beyond limitations and mediocrity. As a Counselor, his purpose is to bring healing to families, shaping thoughts, developing people and organisations to love, serve and to reach for their highest potential.

Reindorf lives in Ghana with his lovely wife Diane and two wonderful boys, Jessey and Jayden-David.

You may encounter many defeats, but you must not be defeated. In fact, it may be necessary to encounter the defeats, so you can know who you are, what you can rise from, how you can still come out of it.

— Maya Angelou

Dedication

Dedicated to my lovely wife Diane for her unending love, to my two wonderful sons Jessey and Jayden-David who give me a reason to live, to Godfred and Gifty my great siblings for their inspiration; to my Mother, Kate, for instructing me to learn till I die; and to Rev. Dr. Mensa Otabil for showing me the way to excellence.

Acknowledgment

I am blessed and highly favoured to be surrounded by people who have had a positive and tremendous impact on my life. Without their sincere encouragement and support, I wouldn't have seen the leader in me. For all who have helped in the shaping of my thoughts, dared me to soar on higher heights, I am truly grateful.

I would like to thank Dr. Cephas Narh for sharing his precious time, knowledge and rich experience throughout the process of writing this book. He has been my motivation.

I particularly owe a debt of gratitude to my inspirational lecturer and Clinical Psychologist,

Mrs Aku Hayfron (Central University College), whose effective comments, criticisms and suggestions greatly helped in shaping my thoughts and stimulating my desire for big dreams. I wish to express my heartfelt gratitude to my team at IntergrityLeadership, Denise, my brainy Executive Assistant, and Kwadwo for their effort and support through the process of writing "The Winning Mind". I also wish to acknowledge the tremendous work of AuthorHouse and all the team members whose relentless effort have made the Publication of "The Winning Mind" a dream come through.

To my wife, Diane for calming my nerves in my tough times and unto the king erternal, the only wise God, for being my source of life.

My past has not defined me, destroyed me, deterred me, or defeated me; it has only strengthened me.

— Steve Maraboli

Do not follow where the path may lead. Go, instead, where there is no path and leave a trail.

—Ralph Waldo Emerson

Preface

"Those who cannot change their minds cannot change anything." My mind expanded when I read this taught provoking quote by George Bernard Shaw. I have discovered that no human being can reach his /her fullest potential without changing his/her way of thinking. "The Winning Mind" is not a Psychology book to bore you with theories. Since Psychology has been widely defined by most writers as "the study of the mind," it becomes necessary for the advancement of humankind.

I am not a psychologist and this book like I said earlier, is not a Psychology book with theories you wouldn't understand. I have discovered that,

Psychology plays part of our everyday life from bed to the time we sleep.

Bishop Noel Jones noted, "Psychology cannot be separated from Theology. Because in every theology there is Psychology. If that were not so, then, Jesus could not require that we be transformed by the renewing of our mind". I believe Psychology helps us to understand our mental processes and behaviours that affect the choices we make and ultimately our lives.

'The Winning Mind' combines Psychological and Biblical principles coupled with simple but profound life lessons I have experienced, applied and has yielded remarkable results for over a decade. I have come to know that, for you to be successful in life you must have control over your mind and develop your mind. Life is not about waiting for chances but creating them. Life is not about giving up when faced with challenges that seem to weigh you down. Life is about fighting and pushing the limit till you win.

This Book is written to hand over to the reader timeless lessons of life, gathered from thirteen years of facing rejection because of my belief in God as well as life transforming principles I have studied from great writers I deeply respect whose life and writings have influenced me to win my way through life.

Robin Sharma, author of 'Megaliving! 30Days to a perfect life' said; *'There are people who make things happen. And there are people who watch things happen. And there are people who say, what happened?'* You were not born to watch but to create.

You will learn proven and tested ways on how to live as a victor and not as a victim.

CHAPTER ONE

Be Different! Rise to the
Place of Excellence.

*Be different so that people can see you clearly amongst
the crowds.*

—Mehmet Murat Ildan

Life is not about repeating what somebody has
already done. It is not about going to the same
places and achieving the same results that people
have experienced already.

That is why you do not have to waste your life trying to be like someone else or trying to do the exact things the heroes of this world have done without paying attention, in order to understand their thinking.

Do Not Become a Clone. There Is a Place for Your Uniqueness.

I believe you have been told that, for you to be successful, you must do exactly what the successful people do. Whereas to some extent this statement can be of great help, it may not be able to help you create your unique self and unearth your own creative abilities. You must learn the thinking processes behind their success, because a man, they say, is a product of his thoughts.

The greatest leader of all times was Jesus Christ, who died and arose on the third day and seated on the right hand side of the Father said, 'Greater works than these shall ye do if you believe in me'. This statement presupposes that we shall not do exactly as Jesus did, but rather something different and something much greater than He did.

You have been created with unique genes and fingerprints peculiar to you alone; therefore, repeating exactly what heroes and exceptional leaders have done will only make you a clone.

The world is seeking to reward originality and integrity. What makes a man excel in this competitive era is not emulating exactly what extraordinary leaders have done, but understanding and learning to think like them.

Dr. Myles Munroe related to this point well when he said, 'If you see me great today, it's because I stood on the shoulders of great people ahead of me'. Wow! Big Idea! Now, let's try this exercise that is designed to enhance your understanding of this profound statement made by Dr. Munroe.

Exercise #1

Please stand up, lift up your eyes and look around from where you are standing. Now write down what you see.

Exercise#2

Please find the second floor of a building and see from that angle. Then, write down what you see. If you were able to do these two simple exercises, you have realized that your perspective at the ground level is limited as compared to your perspective when you are on the second floor of a building.

This is what happens when you learn to understand the thinking processes of the great achievers and successful people. You develop their skill which helps you build upon their knowledge you have acquired in order to create something different from what they did. The world does not benefit anything if you study the thinking of Steve Jobs in order to continue his creation without adding a value in terms of innovation, creativity and style to his inventions. Apple Company does not need CEOs who can think like Steve Jobs but someone who thinks differently, someone who has the leadership to see into the future and can add value to Steve Jobs Legacy he left for the world.

When you live a copy-cat life, you only become a clone and all that you can do is to repeat what people have already done. However, when you learn how great and successful leaders think, you will then develop the ability to create, invent and improve on what they have done.

I have studied and observed two character traits that help successful leaders to make a difference in whatever they do:

- First, they are interested in the formula, not the results. In a classroom, for example, students who are interested in copying answers from their mates end up failing in the exam room. Why?

The answer is obvious: They failed to understand the mathematical principle or the formula that brought about the answer they copied. The student who copies *1+1=2* may fail when given a different figure, such as *2+0=2,* even though the two mathematical equations are derived from the same mathematical principle.

The principle here is this: Successful leaders are always interested in knowing what brings about the answers. They spend time understanding how the principles of life operate. They acquire understanding and then make a difference.

- Second, they are interested in the make-up of a man, not in his achievement.

Every great and successful leader is made up of qualities such as character, attitude, and integrity. To me, these are the factors that produce their success.

To be creative enough to make a difference, you must learn not to be interested in the product but in the process.

In order to be irreplaceable, one must always be different.

—Coco Chanel

Do you wish to stay on top of the game? Do you wish to carve a niche for yourself so well that your organization cannot do without you? Then, be different in the way you think, be different in your attitude and character. Learn to change the old ways of doing things and humbly embrace a new way of doing things to cause new things to happen.

I do not want to be predictable, and I do not want to be replaced. I have observed that the most successful people are unpredictable and irreplaceable in life. This is what gets them winning. They think in order to improvise and constantly develop strategies to keep them in the game of winning.

I urge you not to imitate and learn from what great people have done and just stop there. You have to start where great people ended.

The Power of Adventurous Living

A doctor friend of mine once told me, 'Reindorf, I try to drive through a path I do not know once a week just to know where it may lead me." And this is what she said after I curiously asked why. 'So that I may know where to pass when I am stuck in traffic'.

What are you discovering as a human being? What path are you creating for yourself and the world to follow? What difference are you making with your life?

Prepare, Seize Your Opportunities

Success occurs when opportunity meets preparation.

—Zig Ziglar

I have come to realize that the most unsuccessful people are those who leave life to chance without preparation. Indeed, the Bible says, "Time and chance happeneth to them all" (Eccl 9:11).

What will make you different from another person is your ability to see and seize opportunities that life presents to you, even in the most obscure manner. To make a real difference in life, you need to prepare and train yourself in order to have the leverage necessary to seize any opportunity that comes your way; for no human being can make the best out of the opportunities that come their way without preparation.

Life is about preparation, acquiring self- knowledge and getting ready for the unknown.

You may lose out on great opportunities that could have helped you to climb up the ladder to success simply because you have not prepared yourself for the task.

You are created to make an impact. You are born with the genes of the God that turns mistakes into miracles and bitter experiences into better experiences. You are not here on Earth to imitate and die, but to innovate and live in the minds of people forever.

It is a common experience that a problem difficult at night is resolved in the morning after the committee of sleep has worked on it.

—John Steinbeck

For his anger endureth but a moment; in his favour is life: weeping may endure for a night, but joy cometh in the morning.

—Psalm 30:5(KJV)

CHAPTER TWO

Grow Out of Your Problems

Problems are not stop signs, they are guidelines.

—Robert H. Shuller

Problems are only opportunities in work clothes.

— Henry Kaiser

It was now 6.00 p.m. and I had to take my first-born, Jessey, to see the paediatrician. He was diagnosed with an infection around the respiratory system.

As a new and loving father I was much disturbed by seeing the pain and discomfort my boy had to endure.

To my surprise, during a lengthy discussion with the paediatrician, I learned something profound..

She looked straight into my eyes and upon seeing my troubled heart, she said, 'Sir, please don't worry, your son will be just fine.'

She smiled with surety sparkling in her eyes and added, 'Your son must contract a number of infections so as to help him build resistance against them, which is necessary for his growth.'

'Wow!' I whispered.

Spending time with the paediatrician and paying attention to the wisdom she had to share with me opened up a new understanding of the word 'Problem'. I learnt from this exposure that it is necessary that we go through challenges in order to build resistance against those challenges.

Again, the challenges, the pleasant, unpleasant and the ugly situations we face in life, are there to strengthen us, to stretch us to achieve excellence.

That which does not kill us makes us stronger.

—*Friedrich Nietzsche*

We live in a world where problems are inevitable. You may be asking yourself, 'Why does evil happen to good people?' Why did you go through that divorce? Why did you go through that surgery? You may have experienced some terrible accident that nearly caused your death.

You may have experienced some financial hardship that has led you into owing a heavy debt as an individual or organization. You may have lost someone dear to you.

Whatever your story is, there is always a good purpose behind why things happen the way they do. The challenges you went through or are now going through are never meant to hinder your progress.

Problems rather come to show you the missing *idea* in your life. They come to mature you and carry you into a place called posterity.

Life has taught me that things do not always go as planned.

The loss of a loved one, a career, or other losses, all may seem to be problems. They bring heaviness of heart and all the mixed feelings you can imagine. It's painful! I agree, because I have been there. But I have news for you: Problems when seen as challenges become ladders of opportunities.

Mr. Ashish Kirpal Pandit, the CEO of Fortis Health World Ltd, related to this point well when he said, 'Two things I learnt from my work and real life: to take up challenges and turn them into opportunities. Problems are not stop signs, they are guidelines.' Never see a problem as something that comes to stay but rather as a challenge that is only passing by.

You are gifted to overcome your challenges and master the lessons therein for personal and organizational success.

In his classic article, 'Problems Reveal Genius', Robin Sharma writes, "Problems are servants. They help you grow and lead to better things, both within your organization and in your life. To resist them is to avoid growth and progress. Embrace and get the best from the challenges in front of you and understand that the only people with no problems are dead.'

On the field of battle, what makes the commander win is not running away from the enemy but mustering the courage to confront the enemy.

In life, what gets you at your best is learning to master the art of control in order to keep balance when you find yourself in the storms of life.

Haruki Murakami notes, 'And once the storm is over, you won't remember how you made it through, how you managed to survive. You won't even be sure whether the storm is really over. But one thing is certain. When you come out of the storm, you won't be the same person who walked in. That is what this storm is all about.'

Problems become ladders of opportunities when seen as challenges.

-Reindorf O. Bempah

Stop Thinking *Problem!* Call It *Challenge* and See the Opportunities.

Great and successful leaders have cultivated a habit of seeing problems as opportunities for advancement. In other words, they use their stumbling blocks as building blocks.

Some years back, I used to talk and worry about my challenges. I realize that I created no solutions by doing so. Learning from the thoughts of successful men like Napoleon Hill, the author of *Think and Grow Rich*, Dale Carnegie, Dr. Robert Schuller, as well as the profound teachings of Jesus Christ, the all-knowing and only Begotten Son of God, led me to discover the power of seeing problems as challenges and turning them into possibilities. They relabelled the word *problem* as *challenge*. To me, this is a key that makes life comfortable and much easier.

I have observed that none of these great men had a bad perception about life. In other words, they only saw possibilities and were consumed with the 'can do' spirit and mentality. Their thinking rose above any expression that connotes negativity or impossibility in their world and let them burn all bridges behind them and walk over every mountain that stood in their way.

Their vocabulary never had words like *problem* or *impossible*. In their experiences, problems were seen as challenges and impossibilities as opportunities for possibilities. This establishes the proposition that it is not really a matter of believing that problems exist or not, but it is about a matter of how you see issues of life. I believe strongly that in order to overcome the daily challenges we see in this world, we must rise to a level where we will rise above our world and take off the limit in our thinking.

The Key

Lastly, I must say that there is nothing like *impossible*. And there is also nothing like *can't*.

The secret code here is that these two words already have the solution inside them. Within *impossible* lies the word *possible* and within the word *can't* also lies the word *can*.

What this means is that in life you must not be too quick to see only the problem because every problem comes with a solution.

Think through your challenges and you will discover the amazing solutions embedded in your challenges.

Our life is what our thoughts make it.

—Marcus Aurelius

CHAPTER THREE

Change Your Thoughts and Transform Your Life

Your thoughts are like the seeds you plant in your garden. Your beliefs are like the soil in which you plant these seeds."

—Louise Hay

For as he thinketh in his heart, so is he.

—Proverbs 23:7

Human beings are said to be the sum total of their thought process. Thoughts are seeds, whereas the mind is the soil in which seeds are sown. The soil provides anchor and nutrition for plants to grow and reproduce in large quantities. Farmers only sow what they expect to harvest.

This implies that you will harvest whatever grows from the thoughts (seed) you allow into your mind (soil), whether constructive or destructive.

Every thought-seed sown or allowed to fall into the mind and take root produces its own kind, growing sooner or later into actions, and bearing its own fruit of opportunity and circumstance.

We must understand that whether a man becomes healthy and wealthy will depend on the kind of thoughts he constantly meditates on. Good thoughts bear good fruits, bad thoughts bad fruits.

According to the law of genetics every living thing reproduces after its kind. Jesus said, 'The words that I speak unto you are spirit and life', the implication being that thoughts are living things within our souls. The thought of a man has a dynamic power to manifest what he secretly fears and also what he believes.

Bad Thinking Will Attack Your Progress

One day, I met a dog trainer who was feeding his male Rottweiler. The dog was huge and terrifying to behold.

Though in my mind I feared the dog may attack me, yet I stretched my hands out to touch him and immediately the dog started barking seriously at me.

Another friend came around and gently stretched his hands to touch this same dog and the dog started playing with him.

So I asked why the dog had barked, almost wanting to rip me apart and yet behaved differently towards my other friend. The dog trainer said to me, 'Whenever you come close to a dog and you are full of fear, the dog smells the aura of fear around you and that causes it to attack in order to defend itself. Your friend, on the other hand, came without fear but with a sense of love, showing affection to the dog and so he got affection from the dog.'

Wow! Great idea!

The wisdom in this dog scenario is this: the world belongs to people who are optimistic in their thinking. They defy the old and unprogressive rules of life by constantly being different. They love more and give more, and so more always comes to them.

I believe the difference between me and my other friend is that he gave love and received love whereas I gave fear. In the same manner, as an entrepreneur, whenever you allow the fear of losing an investment to cloud your mind, you will end up losing the investment. Fear will suppress your creative thinking abilities, making it impossible for you to search strategically for solutions. Whenever you cloud your mind with the fear of delivering a speech, you may end up messing up on stage.

Once again, your fear will cripple you from delivering your speech with speed, accuracy, sharpness and awareness of mind. Talk about all the great musicians like Ron Kenoly, Darlene Zscheck of Hillsong fame, Michael Jackson, Whitney Houston, and Stevie Wonder, all of whom could thrill their audiences with such excellent and remarkable performances.

What you probably did not know about them is that each trained in order to overcome stage fright. Are you scared of starting that business? Well do not be; if there is anything to be afraid of, it is your fear and not your vision, goals and aspirations that have the potential of taking you to the top where you belong.

The Mind: Your Most Valuable Asset

Your thoughts form your world. The value of your days is dependent on the richness of your thoughts. I have had the privileged to serve under the ministry of one of Africa's great and world-class leaders, Dr. Mensa Otabil. This man was born without a silver spoon in his mouth yet had a dream that his mind could not get rid off. He learnt to be strong in the mind, envisioning and creating a mental picture of establishing a self-supporting university while pastoring in a classroom. The unpainted walls and broken chairs of the classroom could not resist his passion and desire for creating change. As I stood at the Accra Sports Stadium in Ghana, I listened as he shared this remarkable story of how God took him from nowhere to be the Chancellor of Central University College, one of the leading world-class universities in Africa, and a Senior Pastor of pastors on the thirty-year anniversary of International Central Gospel Church, ICGC, on March 2014. I could only see a man who has fought mediocrity and has developed awareness for change.

His remarkable success story has shown me how far and high I can reach in life. He has challenged me to take the limits off my mind and has dared me to dream big.

He has made me recognize through his life-changing words that I do not need to depend on borrowing from people; rather, if I can reach down to bring out what is inside of me, to create services for the world, I can become anything I wish to be. You too can become the person you wish to be if you can dare yourself to dream big, think big regardless of your present dark situation. The most successful leaders are those who think beyond their limit.

Think Beyond Your Pocket

The successful leaders have a habit I call 'thinking beyond the pocket'. They know that they cannot plan the size of a big dream based on the size of their pocket.

In other words, they believe they do not have to see billions of dollars in their account before they start dreaming big. On the contrary, millions of dollars hit their account *because* they dream big. Most of us will straight ahead think of money first, the very moment we hear words like wealth and success. But the truth is, you do not need money to be successful or wealthy. What you need is an idea; that one thing that you are passionate about is all you need.

This is because money becomes available when there is a vision. One of the winning secrets of success I have learnt in life is that you do not look for money but rather search for the one thing that matters most and do it with all your passion and energy.

One day posterity will find you. The world's wisest and richest man, King Solomon, asserted, 'Whatever your hands find to do, do it with all your might.'

What one thing brings energy and passion into your life that can improve you and the people around you?

Fulfilment in life starts from discovering and focusing all your energies and skill on that one thing that the Creator gave you.

The Power of Focused Thinking

Whenever the human mind is set on one thing it achieves remarkable rewards. Perhaps the greatest failure of mankind is our inability to focus our mind on the things that matter most as far us our existence on Earth is concerned.

I believe each and every one of us is born with a mission to accomplish here on Earth, and to find fulfilment is to execute that one assignment.

Learning to focus your thinking on personal development, organizational growth or goal helps to expose the genius in you. This way of thinking reveals hidden answers for solving complex challenges. Great thinkers like Brian Tracy focused on inventing Microsoft and he did it. Mandela focused on teaching the world about love that brings peace and he did.

Kwame Nkrumah focused on the liberation and independence of Ghana and Africa in general. While some may argue that, he could not bring independence to all African countries by himself, his statement, 'The independence of Ghana is meaningless until the total liberation of Africa' became a driving force for the independence of Africa in general.

All great achievers are known to be focused thinkers. They always are passionate and consumed by a burning desire about one thing that matters most.

The Power of Positive Thoughts

Our life becomes better or worse as our mind goes through the following three steps.

- Things excite our senses and produce thoughts in our conscious mind.

- The thoughts are sent to our subconscious mind where they develop into beliefs.

- The beliefs are mechanically acted on.

This then results in either negative or positive actions.

In Africa, for example, some fathers make statements like 'Why are you so dull, I am just paying school fees for nothing', when they have a little problem with the ward's grades at school.

Now this comment stimulates the conscious mind of the child, causing the child to think, 'I'm dull'. This thought is then transferred to the subconscious where it becomes a belief. The result? Without understanding why, or thinking about it, this child keeps being dull and failing.

The father's comment has become a self-fulfilling prophecy. We are therefore cautioned to be careful of what we say to others and what we say to ourselves.

James Allen said it all when he remarked, 'Mind is the Master, the power that moulds and makes, and Man is Mind, and ever more he takes the tool of thought, and shaping what he wills, brings forth a thousand joys, a thousand ills. He thinks in secret and it comes to pass; environment is but his looking-glass'.

This implies that the human mind has the power to mould and bring into existence every picture of the future it holds. You can actually influence the future based on the kind of thoughts you hold in your mind today. Positive thinking will get you positive results. As I mentioned earlier, thinking is like a farmer sowing seeds. Whatever thought you hold in your mind, be it good or bad, will soon become your reality. If you think like a loser you will become a loser and if you think like a winner, you will win your way out through life no matter your past and current circumstances.

Inside you is a great and creative gift called *mind*. You can create everything you wish for only if you can hold the image and a constant thought of that which you wish for.

Pastor Ed Gungor observed, 'There is power from the mind and people do often become what they think about, but it is incomplete if one does not acknowledge the role that God plays in our everyday lives'.

If you can trust in God and take the time to think about one thing that matters most in your life, all the energies, power and opportunities will be pulled in your direction to help you succeed.

> *Now unto him that is able to do exceeding*
> *abundantly above all that we ask or think,*
> *according to the power that worketh in us.*
>
> *—Ephesians 3:20 KJV*

This scripture supposes that there is power inside of everyone created by God. There is enough power in thinking to create whatever Man desires.

What You Focus on Magnifies

Do you wish to live a healthy life? Then focus on being healthy. Do you wish to see yourself rising as the leader you want to be? Then focus on things pertaining to leadership. People become surgeons, architects, lawyers because of the power of focus. This implies that we have architects because people spent minutes, hours, days, months, and years focusing and studying architecture.

Again, we have medical doctors because people spent minutes, hours, days, months, and years focusing and studying medicine. This does not happen by magic but by focusing on that one thing you want to become.

Using Self-Fulfilling Prophecy to Your Advantage

Self-fulfilling prophecy is a concept developed by Robert K. Merton to explain how a belief or expectation, whether correct or not, affects the outcome of a situation or the way a person (or group) will behave.

Research conducted by Robert Rosenthal and Lenore Jacobson in 1968 proved that the greater the expectations that are put on people the better they will perform. The research involved telling teachers that certain students had higher IQs than others – even though this information was made up. The fact that the teachers believed that certain students had higher abilities than others caused them to interact with these students differently. The outcome was that the scores of the children singled out improved far more than those of other children. (Rosenthal 1995).

I was introduced to this term in my psychology class when learning cognitive therapy at the university. Basically, it means that what you believe will usually happen.

If you believe you are feeling sick, you probably will be sick. If you think people do not like you, you will experience people not liking you. If you believe whatever you do does not come out with good results, so shall it be.

In all these cases, what you are doing is feeding your subconscious mind with worse images and thought patterns that will greatly increase the possibility of their actually happening. Thus, for example, labelling someone a *criminal* and treating that person as such may foster criminal behaviour in the person who is subjected to the expectation. In our own environment we will realize that children who are normally referred to as bad children usually end up being bad.

The reason is that the subconscious mind of the child has picked up the identity of being bad. The result is that the poor child will begin to draw anything that connotes bad into his/her life.

He/she may not be able to live better because of the expectation placed on him/her by his/her environment (parent/guardian).

How It Works

Self-fulfilling prophecy works when you accept what others have sown into you. Secondly, it works when you yourself make a self-destructive statement or have a negative belief concerning a thing, a person or a place.

How I Changed from an Average Student to an Excellent Student

My personal experience was amazing. In the last days of my university education I realized my GPA was not encouraging. I had always thought I was an average student, getting C+ and sometimes B.

One day after a lecture on self-fulfilling prophecy, I decided never again to get a C+. Amazingly, that semester I had A, B and B+ throughout all my papers. What I realized was that, because I refused to accept that I was an average student, I placed a demand on myself to study and do more research work that helped me to pass my exams.

Talk to Yourself

You may have been told by people that you are an average person. You may have accepted that you do not matter or probably see yourself as a tiny little thing just passing through the earth. Today I dare you to start talking to yourself differently. This practice is used by today's successful leaders every day.

Get up from your weeping bed and say to yourself every morning before going out and every evening before going to bed:

I am wealth.
I am good health,
I feel great.
I am above and not beneath.
I am the best
I represent integrity
I am a giver
I lend, I do not borrow

This practice will get your day started in high spirit for great performance as a leader, businessman, or pastor, and with time, you will begin to see your life pleasantly falling into place.

What to Do? It's a Choice.

I believe you have the choice to believe in what other people believe. And is your choice to allow the fears of others to scare you from making informed decisions that can change your life?

Replacement

You can replace those self-destructive thoughts and the fears of others with positive ones. You don't have to live in another man's fear.

If you are the type who thinks you are dull in school, what you have to do is to say to yourself, 'I am an excellent student' and 'I am the best in my class'. Doing this will re-align your subconscious mind to respond to being an excellent student.

This will reconstruct your attitudes, mindset and emotions in accordance with the ways a good student should be and very soon you will become the best amongst the best. You will be undefeated in your field of business. You will become a reference point of success.

Mahatma Gandhi nailed it well when he said, 'If you change yourself you will change your world. If you change how you think then you will change how you feel and what actions you take. The world around you will change. Not only because you are now viewing your environment through new lenses of thoughts and emotions but also because the change within can allow you to take action in ways you wouldn't have or maybe even have thought about – while stuck in your old thought patterns'.

It is said, 'He that cannot change his thinking cannot change anything.' I urge you to embrace a change in your thinking to positively transform your life and make a difference wherever you find yourself.

The central fire is desire, and all the powers of our being are given us to see, to fight for, and to win the object of our desire. Quench that fire and man turns to ashes.

-Basil W. Marturin

THREE KEYS USED BY
GREAT ACHIEVERS

CHAPTER FOUR

Key #1

The Power of Desire

Therefore I say unto you, what thingsoever ye desire, when ye pray, believe that ye receive them, and ye shall have them.

—Jesus Christ

By believing passionately in something that does not yet exist, we create it. The nonexistent is whatever we have not sufficiently desired".

—Nikos Kazantzakis

According to Wikipedia, desire is a sense of longing or hoping for a person, object, or outcome. The same sense is expressed by terms such as 'craving' and 'hankering'.

When a person desires something or someone, their sense of longing is excited by the enjoyment of the thought of the item or person, and they want to take action to obtain their goal.

The motivational aspect of desire has long been noted by philosophers; Thomas Hobbes (1588–1679) asserted that human desire is the fundamental motivation of all human action. This chapter seeks to introduce you to the three keys that make successful people win.

Desire is one of the most powerful keys for achieving whatever a man needs. Without desire for something, nothing comes into existence. To live without desire in this world is to live a life of lack and unfulfilment.

Look around you; all the people you see in high offices got there as a result of their desire. Leaders emerge because of desire. Desire is said to be the first step in the creation process.

God created the world and everything in it out of His desire to create man and enjoy the company and worship of his creation. In this life, we were all created to be successful, creative and innovative beings.

Make a Choice to Desire Change

I believe we were created to be great fathers, great leaders, great husbands and wives. Unfortunately, some choose to fail while others choose to win.

The truth is that the successful people we see around us make certain choices and do some things that the unsuccessful ones do not.

People become presidents because of their innate desire for effecting a change, achieving something or becoming something.

Using the Magnetic Force of Desire to Your Advantage

Desire may be likened to a magnetic energy field that possesses the ability to pull to you whatsoever you need. All you need is a burning desire. You must be very careful of the kind of desire you allow into your heart since you can attract either bad or good, based on the kind of desire you possess. Again, whatever you desire, you must believe you can attain.

And as you believe and desire passionately, those things that you desire will find their way into your life. Have you ever desired something you did not have, and after having that thought for a while, that which you desired came to you?

Burt Goldman, in his book *The Power of Mind Control*, emphasizes the three mighty forces of power – desire, belief, and expectation.

According to Goldman, before anything you want to happen can occur, you must desire that it happens. You must believe that it can happen. And you must expect it to happen.

This means that in order for you to see the future unfolding, you must first of all desire, believe and more importantly be in constant expectancy. You must expect earnestly like the pregnant woman expects her unborn child with hope and faith.

Rob Willis notes that 'it is desire that is the driving force to help you get what you want in life. Man needs the kind of desire that has him thinking about his purpose constantly'. He continues to say that it is only when desire to achieve consumes your every waking moment that you will start to move forward.

Desire Does Not Fail

It is this sort of desire that turns dreams into reality. Desire forces you into action to follow your dreams. It is desire that will see you through the hard times when all looks lost. Desire does not understand failure. Desire will find the way to help you achieve your purpose.

CHAPTER FIVE

Key #2

The Wisdom of Goal-Setting

Setting goals is the first step in turning the invisible into the visible.

—Tony Robbins

Everyone in life must be guided by goals. Studies have proven that people who set goals do better than those who do not, but few people really understand the influence of goal-setting in life. King Solomon observed, 'A man's gift maketh room for him, and bringeth him before great men.

Learn to commit to your goals and your gifts will take you places that will surprise you.'

In my view, a goal is a person's mental outlook on how he wants the future to be. I believe goal-setting is inevitable in a person's pursuit of success. Without goals, we are likely to live without guide.

One must understand that without goals there is no direction and without direction there is no destination.

Plan for Your Goals

Pablo Picasso observed, 'Our goals can only be reached through a vehicle of a plan, in which we must fervently believe, and upon which we must vigorously act. There is no other route to success.' It is said that "goals that are not written down are just wishes'. For goals to come alive we must learn the discipline of writing and planning our goals.

It may be a goal for a week, a year or even a twenty-year long-term goal. All it takes for it to manifest is your determination to work towards the achievement of your goal little by little. For it is said, 'little drops of water makes a mighty ocean'.

Choosing to Win Each Day through Goal-Setting

It is said that goals and visions are deliberate choices we make in an attempt to define the direction of our lives.

However, I believe the worst tragedy that can happen to a man is for him to think that he has nothing to offer, no choice and no control over life.

While it may be true that there are things beyond your direct control, it is not what happens to you that matters, but the choices you make concerning what happens to you.

Aristotle defined choice as 'deliberate desire with the heart providing the passion and the head, the reason. When we make decisions based solely on logic, they lack meaning and seem vacuous.'

We must understand that the choices we make in our challenging moments are what determine our tomorrow.

Imagination is the beginning of creation. You imagine what you desire, you will what you imagine, and at last you create what you will.

—George Bernard Shaw

CHAPTER SIX

Key #3

Imagination

Now unto him that is able to do exceeding abundantly above all that we ask or think, according to the power that worketh in us.

—Apostle Paul

Imagination rules the world.

—Napoleon Bonaparte

According to Norman Vincent Peale, imagination is one of the greatest laws of the universe. However, it is a pity that it has been misunderstood.

Imagination is neither an occult practice nor evil. It is a power God placed in us so that we may function like Him. Imagination came into being the very day God created the world and Man. Imagination is the womb of creation.

This universe and Man existed in the imagination of God. As God's children, we use imagination every day of our lives either consciously or unconsciously.

We use imagination whenever we plan an event, whenever the architect designs a building, whenever the artist paints a picture, and whenever we plan what to wear.

Napoleon Hill notes that 'imagination is literally the workshop wherein are fashioned all plans created by men. The impulse, the desire, is given shape, form, and action through the aid of the imaginative faculty of the mind'. He continues, asserting that Man can create anything that the mind can imagine. Imagination is one of God's gifts to mankind to help shape lives and destinies. It is a great power that has the potency to change one's entire life of misery and conduct one into a new world of success.

The Creative Power of Imagination

Invention is the product of imagination. Do you know that all the great inventions we can see now in our world such as airplanes, cars, light bulbs, telephones, etc., were created out of the power of imagination? All that has been invented by great minds like Steve Jobs, George Edward Alcorn, Bill Gates, etc., were things that preoccupied their imaginative faculties as a result of their pursuit to solve a problem so as to meet human needs. So now, what is it that you cannot achieve? It is all within your reach. All you need to do is to:

1. Form a clear, consistent and definite picture of your future and take daily steps in the direction of your imagined goal.
2. Desire to see what you have imagined in your mind made manifest

3. Believe that you are already in possession and take personal responsibility towards the attainment of whatever it is that you have imagined

Imagination brings about an action plan for our goals and visions in life. In other words, it will cause you to act on whatever image you hold in your mind.

Imagination Will Buy the Future at No Cost

At some point in my life at the junior high school I have imagined myself continuing my senior high school education at Kumasi Senior High School, one of the best colleges in Ghana.

When the time was up for freshmen admissions, my records were nowhere to be found for some strange reason. At that moment my dreams seemed impossible since without those records I could not be admitted. I stayed home for three months while my colleagues proceeded to the various senior high schools of their choice. In spite of all these challenges I kept on imagining myself seated right in my Visual Arts class, learning with my friends at the very school I had always desired.

Sometimes, I visualized myself on the bed in my dormitory. Other times, I imagined myself at the library learning.

I kept on doing this till one day my childhood friend's father called me, took me by the hand and sent me to another high school that I was not interested in, just to look for other ways of helping me get enrolled, and yet it did not work out.

I went back to my desired senior high school and as I was walking and desiring the environment, I met a student who knew me. He had seen me playing piano at a conference. He led me into the office of the Headmaster and right there the man authorised me to be admitted with immediate effect. To cut the story short, I got admission through this student. Finally, my imagination had brought about the future.

In this life, you can achieve anything that your mind can imagine. You don't need to worry about the money. All you need to do is to have a mental picture of what you really, really need or desire and it will find its way into your life.

This is because desire has the ability to bring men to a place where their thoughts are moulded into a strategic plan that places a demand on the object desired to cause its release into the physical.

God is able to answer not only that which you ask of Him but more, that which you imagine.

Author Napoleon Hill asserted, 'Whatever the mind can conceive and believe, it can achieve'.

How to Live Beyond the Limit

George Bernard Shaw observed, 'Imagination is the beginning of creation. You imagine what you desire, you will what you imagine and at last you create what you will.' Look around and you'll see that this is true. The world has recorded a number of inventions and great epic stories all through imagination. Can we create our ideal future regardless of our individual challenges and live beyond the limits we find ourselves in? Amy Purdy's story can answer that question.

Amy M. Purdy (born 1979) is an American actress, model, world-class snowboarder and 2014 Paralympic Bronze Medallist, co-founder of Adaptive Action Sports, professional motivational speaker, clothing designer, author and dancer.

At age nineteen, she contracted neisseria meningitis, a form of bacterial meningitis. The disease affected her circulatory system when the infection led to septic shock; both of her legs had to be amputated below the knee, she lost both kidneys, and her spleen was removed.

Sepsis is when an infection causes a system-wide inflammatory response, leading to organ failure and/or clinical shock, and is a common cause of death. In Purdy's case, she went into septic shock within twenty-four hours of getting sick. Doctors gave her only a 2 per cent chance to survive since her sepsis was so advanced. Two years later, she received a kidney transplant from her father.[1]

Amy Purdy had lived a 'normal' childhood and spent her high school years as a passionate artist and snowboarder.

After losing her legs, she has persevered, taking on great challenges and rising above them.

I was thrilled as I watched her say these words on the TED platform: 'If you ask me today if I would want to change my situation, I would say no because my missing legs have not disabled me. If anything, they have enabled me, they have forced me to rely on my imagination and to believe in possibilities'. She explains, 'Our imaginations can be used as tools for breaking through borders, because in our minds we can do anything, and we can be anything'. Today, Amy is an athlete, currently the top-ranked adaptive female snowboarder in the world. She also spends a good amount of time serving others, particularly those with bodily

---

[1]   http://en.wikipedia.org/wiki/Amy_Purdy

challenges, helping them to learn snowboarding, skateboarding, wakeboarding and other action sports through the organization she co-founded, Adaptive Action Sports – challenging herself while making a positive impact on the world.

'Our obstacles can only do two things: one, stop us in our tracks, two, force us to get creative', says Amy Purdy.

I have realized that in life, in order for you to get to the next level, you have to face and conquer your fears and consciously train your mind to clearly paint the picture of the future you desire and not as you see your current situation.

Your immediate situation might be nothing to write home about. It may be a poor image to behold. It may be a situation filled with sickness and sorrow.

If you can imagine a life full of vitality, sound mind, wealth, and good health, you will one day be living in your imagination.

Pablo Picasso nailed it well when he said, 'I paint objects as I think them, not as I see them'.

I dare you to take your eyes off your limits and start painting a future without limit.

At the end of life we will not be judged by how many diplomas we have received, how much money we have made, how many great things we have done.

We will be judged by 'I was hungry, and you gave me something to eat, I was naked and you clothed me. I was homeless, and you took me in'.

—Mother Teresa

CHAPTER SEVEN

What You Make Happen for Others Will Happen to You

Do unto others as you would have them do unto you.

—Jesus Christ of Nazareth

Human beings are naturally selfish. It is an innate nature of men to be selfish, putting ourselves and our desires first before others. It is natural to want to have a bite of the cake first. It seems okay to want to have the last portion of the bread on the family dining table all to yourself without any remorse. Our minds have been unconsciously trained to be selfish and unfortunately we take this same attitude into the workplace, church, and marriage, thereby ruing the very relationships that were meant to get us to the top.

People are seeking to be great leaders, good entrepreneurs, and good husbands and yet they lack this simple rule of life: serve others. I have observed that the road to the top is to serve others.

Learning to put others first is not an act of self-abuse. It's a gift you give yourself that will pay off one day. Jesus Christ of Nazareth asserted, 'He who wishes to be great must serve'. I have heard many times people saying, 'You do not have to live in someone else's vision.' On the contrary, I have learnt that in life it is not all of us who are called to be the pioneers of a vision but rather some people's vision that will be helping another person's vision come through.

Maybe you were not called to stand alone but to stand by the side of another to help turn their dreams into reality, and together make your world a better place. The highly successful people understand what it means to serve and give a helping hand.

This is because they have understood the value in emptying themselves of their pride and position and have learnt to put people first.

The Golden Rule: A Sure Way for Winning

The biblical phrase 'Do unto others as you would have them do unto you' is known as the Golden Rule. It is well recognized and widely used by most of the world's religions for resolving conflict.

The Golden Rule, which is also known as the ethic of reciprocity, has its roots in a wide range of world cultures. Greg M. Epstein notes, '"Do unto others" is a concept that essentially no religion misses entirely'. Simon Blackburn also states that the Golden Rule can be 'found in some form in almost every ethical tradition'. All versions and forms of the proverbial Golden Rule have one aspect in common: They all demand that people treat others in a manner in which they themselves would like to be treated.

The Winning Habit of Celebrating Others

Author Zig Zigler observed, 'You can have everything in life you want, if you will just help enough other people get what they want'. Life is not about selfishness, it's about selflessness. The road to success is not a path of selfishness but a path of selflessness.

Do you want to be appreciated? Find someone to appreciate first. Do you want to be recognized as a great leader, a pastor, a CEO of an organization, then hear this: Learn to deeply recognize people. Doing this genuinely as a leader makes the people you work with feel great and it also vitalizes their energy to perform.

In the end they will give you back in great measure, running over, shaking together the love and the recognition you gave them. People who celebrate others are also celebrated. This is it! That is how the rule works.

There are no short-cuts. If you make people happy, they will love to be around you and they will also automatically make you happy.

You want to be celebrated as the hero of your company, or as a pastor? The question is, when was the last time you celebrated someone?

The road to success is not a path of selfishness but a path of selflessness.

-Reindorf O. Bempah

Life Is About Service

I have a favourite restaurant. One day I was using the washroom when I saw the manager mopping the floor. I looked at him with surprise on my face, wondering "Why on Earth would a manager do this?"

He smiled and said, 'I hope this place is clean enough, sir.'

Life is not about positions and holding big titles, nor is leadership. The essence of life is serving others. I have observed that Life has a way of rewarding people who truly serve their organisation, nation and family. To me, the real meaning of life is revealed in service.

Sayeed, the manager of my favourite restaurant, loves to help and serve customers in any way he can. He believes in teamwork to achieve one goal.

Today in business, some are bound by their positions, from bank managers to CEOs to pastors. When was the last time you stepped out of your air-conditioned office to help customers in the queue as a bank manager?

As a pastor how many times have you stood at the entrance of your church just to say hello while receiving your cherished church members?

This practice will not only make you the best leader but most importantly, it will make you a better person and also make the people you work with love you and be willing to die for you. Doing this genuinely as a leader makes the people you work with feel great and develop energy for peak performance.

I believe the only meaningful evidence of our existence is not the nice cars we drive, or the spectacular mansion we build, but how well we serve others.

You cannot rise above your thinking level. You can only rise to the level of your thinking.

-Reindorf O. Bempah

www.ingramcontent.com/pod-product-compliance
Lightning Source LLC
Chambersburg PA
CBHW050410290526
45786CB00003B/1198